Rookie
Read-About® Math

# How Heavy Is It?

## By Brian Sargent

**Consultant**
Ari Ginsburg
Math Curriculum Specialist

Children's Press®
A Division of Scholastic Inc.
New York   Toronto   London   Auckland   Sydney
Mexico City   New Delhi   Hong Kong
Danbury, Connecticut

Designer: Herman Adler Design
Photo Researcher: Caroline Anderson
The photo on the cover shows a girl lifting a heavy pumpkin.

**Library of Congress Cataloging-in-Publication Data**

Sargent, Brian, 1969–
  How heavy is it? / by Brian Sargent.
     p. cm. — (Rookie read-about math)
  Includes index.
  ISBN 0-516-25267-4 (lib. bdg.)                0-516-25368-9 (pbk.)
  1. Weights and measures—Juvenile literature. I. Title. II. Series.
  QC90.6.S27 2005
  530.8—dc22                                    2005004625

CHILDREN'S PRESS, and ROOKIE READ-ABOUT®,
and associated logos are trademarks and/or registered trademarks
of Scholastic Library Publishing. SCHOLASTIC and associated logos
are trademarks and/or registered trademarks of Scholastic Inc.

1 2 3 4 5 6 7 8 9 10 R 14 13 12 11 10 09 08 07 06 05

# Have you ever carried something heavy?

Did you wonder what
it weighed?

Everything can be
weighed. Weight is how
heavy something is.

Elephants weigh a lot.
Birds weigh very little.
Even air weighs something!

5

You can weigh things
on a scale.

You can weigh fruits
and vegetables in a
grocery store.

How much will you pay
for them? You can weigh
them to find out.

You can weigh letters at the post office. Then you know how many stamps to use.

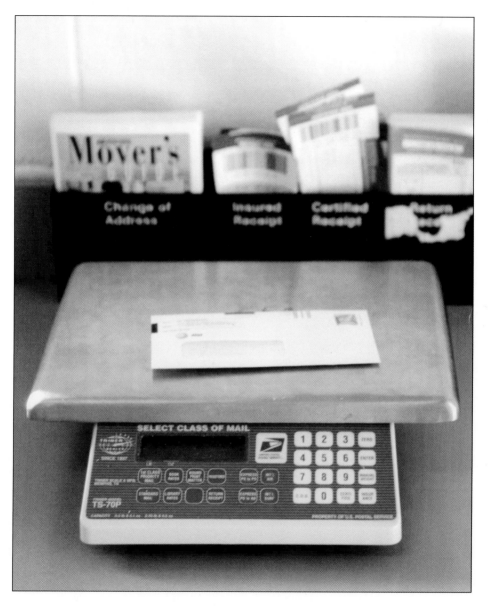

9

10

Truck drivers must be very careful about weight.

Trucks carry heavy loads. A truck that weighs too much may not be safe.

You measure weight with
a scale. There are many
types of scales.

This scale is called
a balance.

13

Let's say you have an orange and an apple.

A balance can tell you which one weighs more than the other.

The basket that holds the heavier fruit will drop.

Weight can be measured in pounds. Sometimes people write "pound" as "lb."

A pound is about as heavy as this loaf of bread.

Light objects are measured in ounces. Sixteen ounces equals 1 pound.

Sometimes people write "ounce" as "oz." An ounce is about as heavy as this slice of bread.

Objects that are very heavy are measured in tons. There are 2,000 pounds in 1 ton.

A small car weighs a little more than 1 ton.

Sometimes things are
measured in pounds
and ounces.

This jar of jelly weighs
1 pound and 2 ounces.
That's a little more than
a pound.

Weight can be very important.

A nurse checks your weight at the doctor's office. She wants to see how much weight you have gained.

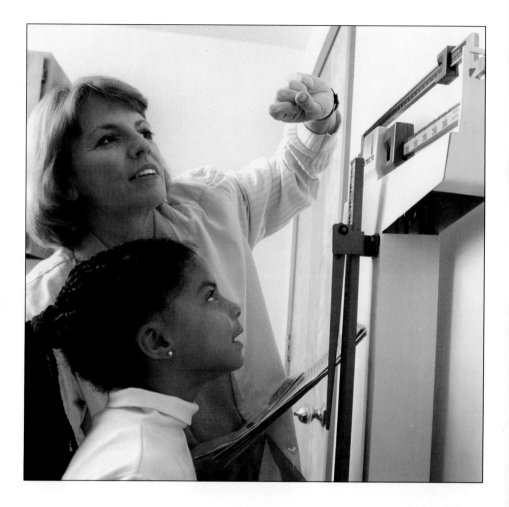

25

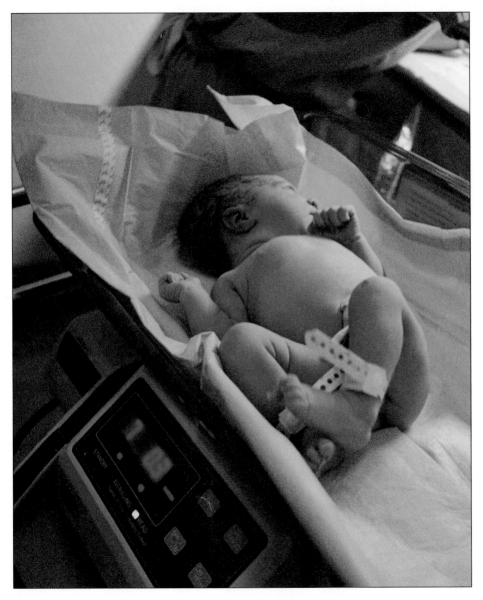

Doctors weigh babies
when they are born.

Weighing a baby helps the
doctor know that the baby
is healthy.

Most babies weigh about
7 pounds when they
are born.

How heavy are you?

Weigh yourself and
find out!

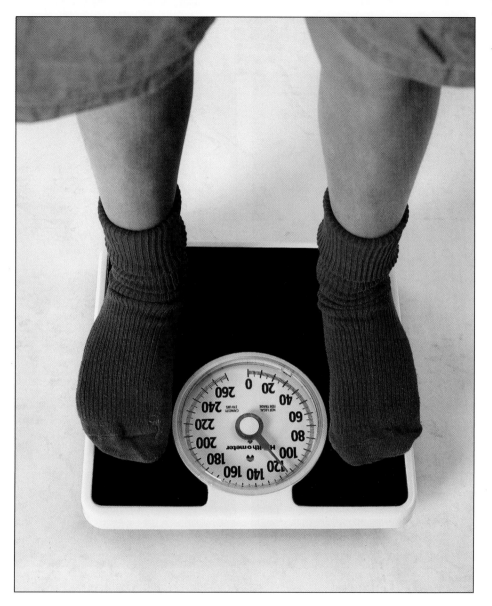

# Words You Know

balance

bread

car

elephant

heavy

scale

truck

weigh

# Index

# About the Author

Brian Sargent is a middle-school math teacher. He lives in Glen Ridge, New Jersey, with his wife, Sharon, and daughter, Kathryn. He weighs 155 pounds.

# Photo Credits

Photographs © 2005: Corbis Images: 26 (Cat Gwynn), 29, 31 bottom right (Richard Hutchings), cover (Royalty-Free), 25 (Tom Stewart); Getty Images/Burke/Triolo Productions/brand x Pictures: 14, 30 top left; ImageState/Image Source: 18; Masterfile: 21, 30 bottom left (K. Hackenberg-Zefa), 10, 31 bottom left (Roy Ooms); Peter Arnold Inc./Martin Harvey: 5, 30 bottom right; PhotoEdit: 3, 31 top left (Jeff Greenberg), 9, 22 (Michael Newman), 6, 31 top right (David Young-Wolff); Superstock, Inc.: 17, 30 top right; The Image Works/David Lassman: 13.